CULINARY SCHOOLS, CLASSES, AND SCHOLARSHIPS

CULINARY SCHOOLS, CLASSES, AND SCHOLARSHIPS

Steve Volk

AuthorHouse™
1663 Liberty Drive
Bloomington, IN 47403
www.authorhouse.com
Phone: 1-800-839-8640

Published by AuthorHouse   03/05/2013

ISBN: 978-1-4817-0347-5 (sc)
ISBN: 978-1-4817-0348-2 (e)

Library of Congress Control Number: 2013900232

Culinary Schools, Classes, And Scholarships
By ADOLPH STEVE VOLK CEPC/CCE/AAC/ & RBA MASTER BAKER

Before You Shelf This Book Away Pass It On To Someone In Need
To Someone Who Is Unemployed, With Very Low Pay, Or Welfare.
Military Veterans Hospital, (Rehabilitation), For Vet. Employment
High School Students Who Can Use A Culinary Scholarship Today
Programs Loaves And Fishes For The Unemployed Needing Skills
Anyone Of Our Four Culinary Books, May Be The Needed Helper

These Books Have Different Levels Of Training, For Those
That Are Unsure. Go Thru This Book, Step By Step.

Go To Book Title (For Culinary Teachers, Students, Chefs,
Bakers, Caterers, Hobbyist, & Unemployed) $22.60 + s/h
Call, Author House, Phone, (1-888-519-5121=Ext. # 5023)

Go To (Bakers Hand Craft Training School,) In Full Color,
Students Baking, Bread, Pastries, Cake Decorating Designs
They Also Learn About Ice Carving,& Pull & Blown Sugar
Culinary Students, From Around The World, Participating
In The 1988 Culinary Olympics. All Below The Age Of 23

Never Let Anyone Make Remarks, About Your Planning On Going
To A Culinary School. The Factories, Banks,& Stores, (May Close)
Leaving Many Millions Of Workers Unemployed, Or On Welfare ?
With Newer Restaurants, Hotels, Clubs, Ships, (Chefs Are Needed)
For Government, The Rich & Famous. Privet Chefs Are In Demand

Chefs Are Needed Teaching In Culinary Schools, Also Jr. Collages
Executive Leveled Chefs Do Ice Carvings, And Center Food Trays
Executive Pastry Chefs, Wedding Cakes, Pull & Blown Sugar Art
Everyday Chefs With Retirement,(They Just Seem To Fade Away)

One Of These Books, Would Make A Nice Gift, For Some One.
My Very Best To Your Future,
adolphstevevolk@yahoo.com

The Retail Bakers of America and its Officers and Directors hereby certify that

Adolph (Steve) Volk

has successfully fulfilled the requirements for designation as a Master Baker under the RBA Master Baker Certification Program.

June 1981

Hans B. Madler
President

Richard C. Gobler
Executive Vice President

Richard M. Stern, Jr.
Chairman, Apprenticeship &
Training Committee

- The Bible does not say whether people used knives, forks, or spoons when eating a meal. It does refer to eating bread which had been dipped into the food (John 13:26). is likely that everyone at the meal dipped their bread into a common pot which held the stew, beans, soup, etc. where, how, and what the people of the Bible ate and drank.
- Sitting on the ground. An animal skin or piece of leather was used to cover the ground The food was placed in the middle of the skin or piece of leather.
- The two main meals were at noon (Genesis 43:16) and in the evening (John 13:2).

Barley (Ruth 1:22)	Cucumbers (Num. 11:5)	Pistachio nuts (Gen. 43:11)
Flax (Ex. 9:31)	Melons (Num. 11:5)	Almonds (Gen. 43:11)
Millet (Ezek. 4:9)	Leeks (Num. 11:5)	Mint (Matt. 23:23)
Spelt (Ezek. 4:9)	Onions (Num. 11:5)	Dill (Matt. 23:23)
Wheat (Gen. 30:14)	Garlic (Num. 11:5)	Cummin (Matt. 23:23)
Wheat bread (Ex. 29:2)	Beans (2 Sam. 17:28)	Sweet cane (Jer. 6:20)
Barley bread (2 Kings 4:42)	Lentils (2 Sam. 17:28)	Cinnamon (Ex. 30:23)
Millet bread (Ezek. 4:9)	Bitter herbs (Ex. 12:8)	Grapes (Deut. 23:24)
Spelt bread (Ezek. 4:9)	Wine (Gen 9:21)	Grape juice (Num. 6:3)
Unleavened bread (Gen. 19:3)	Vinegar (Ruth 2:14)	Raisins (1 Sam. 30:12)
Leavened bread (Matt. 16:12)	Olive oil (Ez. 16:19)	Figs (1 Sam. 30:12)
Pomegranates (Num. 20:5)	Apples (Song of Songs 2:5)	Dates (2 Sam. 6:19)
Lamb (Ex. 12:4)	Ox (Deut. 14:4)	Goat (Deut. 14:4)
Deer (Deut. 14:5)	Gazelle (Deut. 14:5)	Ibex (Deut. 14:5)
Antelope (Deut. 14:5)	Roe Deer (Deut. 14:5)	Wild Goat (Deut. 14:5)
Mountain sheep (Deut. 14:5)	Fish (Num. 11:5)	Locusts (Matt. 3:4)
Honey (Matt. 3:4)	Partridge (1 Sam. 26:20)	Quail (Num. 11:31)
Cricket (Lev. 11:22)	Grasshopper (Lev. 11:22)	Chicken (Matt. 23:37)
Milk (Gen. 18:8)	Curds (Gen. 18:8)	Cheese (2 Sam. 17:29)
Eggs (Job 6:6)	Salt (Job 6:6)	Coriander seeds (Ex. 16:31)
Mustard (Matt. 13:31)	Manna (Ex. 16:31)	Water (Ex. 17:6)

Award-winning Chef and Instructor Releases Guidebook
Seasoned chef instructor delivers book that combines recipes and career advice

FAIR OAKS, Calif. — "For more years than I can to remember, my goal has been to teach the basics in culinary art and food service," remarks chef instructor and author Adolph Volk, who was recently accepted into the American Academy of Chefs. "As a vocational educator I thoroughly enjoyed teaching the culinary profession. From the basics to the skilled, new ideas are never ending and certainly not boring."

Ice, Snow, Sand & Wood Sculptures
Adolph (Steve) Volk

#1
ICE, SNOW, SAND, WOOD, SCULPTURES, 500 PHOTOS
LEARN HOW ITS DONE & CHECK ON COMPETITION

Store List Price $46.25, Author House $29.00, You Save $17.25
Basic Ice Carving Classes, Bakers Hand Craft Training School.
Utah Ice Festival Olympics, & The Chicago Ice Carving Events
See How They Snow Sculpture, & (International Championship)
Master Sand Sculptures, (Single Or Teams), From World Wide
Learn How Its Done, With Only Water, No Binders Are Added
Sacramento Fair, Harrison Lake Canada, Carmel Monterey CA.
Also For Children And Adults Trying Artisic Skills By The Sea
Blanchard, (Itsyville) Wood Sculptures, 667 Hy.68, Salinas CA.

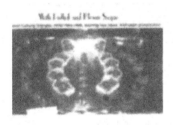

#2
CULINARY OLYMPICES, 1976/84/88/, 400 PHOTOS
PULLED SUGAR LESSONS, CULINARY CHEF TRAYS

Store List Price $46.25, Author House $29.00, You Save $17.25
Pulled And Blown Sugar, Recipes, And Step By Step Lessons
Hands On Instructors, Peter Boyal, Ewald Notter, Pastry Wiz
U.S. Chefs Competitions, Striving For Quality Under Pressure
Center Displays Including, Ice, Tallow, Chocolate, Sculptures
Military Teams World Wide, Cook Under Military Conditions
Culinary Olympic Students, World Wide, Below The Age Of 23
Looking For A New Skill & Employment, Trade Schools Help
Imfo., Call The American Culinary Federation, 800-624-9458

#3
RECIPES & MORE, (400 RECIPES) (500 PHOTOS)
STUDENTS, ICES, CAKE CLUBS, MILITARY, 468 PG.

Store List Price $138.99 Author House $71.50 You Save $67.49
Our Granddaughters, At 13 Worked After School In Our Bakery
Palmiter High School, Vocational Education (Cooking Classes)
San Juan High School, Vocational Education, (Baking Classes)
Lets Prevent School Drop Outs, With (Trade And Skill Classes)
Our Senior Chefs Just Fade Away, Replace Them With Training
Its Time To Train The Unemployed, For New Trades And Skills
Go To A Library, To Research (For Scholarships & Student Aid)

Culinary Trade Schools, Scholarships & Grants
By ADOLPH STEVE VOLK - (ACF) CEPC/ CCE/ AAC / (RBA) Master Baker

How To Upgrade Your Trade & Culinary Skills

For CULINARY TEACHERS, STUDENTS, CHEFS, MIXERS, CATERERS, HOBBYIST, & UNEMPLOYED

How To Upgrade Your Trade & Culinary Skills / How This Book I Might Help

#4   With The Aid Of These Culinary Books Each Book, Has A Different Skill Level.

Store List Price, $41.49./Author House $22.60, You Save $18.89
In This Book #4 Go To, (Bakers Hand Craft Training School)
These Student Were Unemployed & Needed A Trade For Work.
This Was A SETA Program, Backed By (Bakers Union # 85 At
7125 Governors Circle Suite A, Sacramento, California 95823)
The Training, By Founder, Head Baker Supervisor Jim Knowles
Also / Certified Executive Pastry Chef, & Educater, Steve Volk
The Training Was For 6 Months, Mon Thru Friday, 8 Am - 4Pm
The School Was Free To Those In Need Of Acquiring This Skill
For Employment In The Field Of Baking, Pastry, & Culinary Art
In Bake Shops, Stores, Hotels, Clubs, Ships, Catering./ Teaching
In Adult Education, High Schools, Jr. Collages, Culinary Schools,
Orientation & Objectives./Safety & Sanitation./Personal Hygiene,
Art Of Bread & Pastery Baking./Cakes & Icing, Cake Decorating,
Birthdays, Engagement, Wedding, Anniversary, & Baby Shower,
Recipes./ Ice Carving, Butter & Tallow Sculpture, Pulled Sugar
3 Classes, Cake Decorating, Ginger Bread Houses, Ice Carvings

mary Trade Schools, Scholarships & Grants
ADOLPH STEVE VOLK (ACF) CEPC/ CCE/ AAC/(RBA) Master Baker
To Upgrade Your Trade & Culinary Skills

#1 Sculptures, #2 Recipes & More #3 Pulled Sugar,
#4 (Best Book) Bakers Hand Craft Training School
#5 Affairs, Culinary Oversite Student, And Classes.

#5 Culinary Memberships, & Scholarships

For Culinary Introduction   Author House E- Book B/W $13.95
RBA Membership To Success Thru bro@retailbakersofamerica.org
American Culinary Federation Students Education acfchefs.org
American Academy Of Chefs & Sizzle Check ACF Scalorships
The Women Chefs And Restaurateurs, / www.womenchefs.org
National Restaurant Educational Foundation, / www.nraef.org
Prostrate National Certificate Of Achievement /Students, N.R.A.
Henry Ford Community Collage, Ice Carving Club hfccice.com
Alice Connelly Enterprises Ice Carving Crafters-icecrafter.com
International Cake Exploration Society, To Join, www.ice.org
California Cake Club, Batter Chatter, 3C www.cacskeclub.org
For Your Family, Career, And Life / scholarships4moms.net
Minority Scholarships, For Culinary Schools / eltow.con
Quartermaster Culinary Food Service School, At Fort Lee VA.
Go To Culinary Trade Shows & Conventions For New Ideas.
To Order Books Call AuthorHouse, 1-888-519-5121 Ext. 5023

Please Pass This Book To Someone Who Is In Need (Unemployed)
Low Wages,/State Aid./School Drop Out,/ Disabled Vet./ With Very
Little Training Or Skills, These Were My Best Student For Over 50
Years Of Teaching & Working With (My Books Might Help Them)

5

What Is the American Culinary Federation (ACF)?

ACF is the largest and most prestigious chefs' organization in America. We have over 72 years of leadership and education experience in the professional foodservice industry.

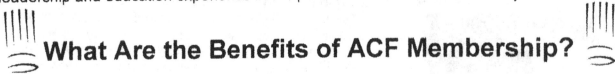

What Are the Benefits of ACF Membership?

- **Toll-free** member assistance through our Member Services Center - 800-624-9458
- **Free** access to our Internet JobBank for members to post their resumes or to review resumes on behalf of their establishments
- **Free** national monthly, cutting-edge publication; *The National Culinary Review*, (NCR)
- **Free** national monthly newsletter; *The Center of the Plate*, included inside the pages of the *NCR*
- **Free** Vendor Resource Guide - a virtual trade show on the ACF Web site
- **Complimentary** Term Life Insurance
- **Automatic** membership in the World Association of Cooks' Societies (WACS)
- **Discounted prices** on Certification (earned) as Professional Chef, Pastry Chef, or Culinary Educator
- **Discounted prices** on ACF Regional Conference and National Convention registrations and room rates
- **Discounted rates** on Alamo Rental Cars
- **Subsidized** ChefTrac Program -- chapter-based required courses for certification
- **Access** to educational grants for professional chef members
- **Notification** of national, regional, and local seminars, workshops, and symposiums
- **Professional networking opportunities** at local, regional, national, and international levels
- **Access** to a no annual fee platinum credit card that supports ACF.

What Else Can You Tell Me About ACF?

- ACF has an easy-to-use Web site (**www.acfchefs.org**) where you can find information on everything from education courses to the International Culinary Olympics.
- The **ACF Chef and Child Foundation** is the philanthropic component of ACF and works to educate young children about proper nutrition and to bring childhood nutrition needs to the attention of those who can help.
- ACF has an honor society - the **American Academy of Chefs.** Long-term membership in ACF is one of many requirements to become a member of this elite group of chefs.

The true impact of ACF membership comes from your participation with the local chapter. Meetings and events can springboard you to new professional horizons.

The American Academy of Chefs

Our mission is to promote education of culinarians. Their success is our future

For more years than I care to remember my goal has been to teach the basics in culinary art and food service. This includes the unemployed, high school dropout or unskilled people who have a desire to better their lives.

Congratulations on your acceptance into the American Academy of Chefs! Each year at the American Culinary Federation's National Convention, the AAC holds its annual dinner where we present the outstanding individuals, who through their dedication to this profession, have made all those contributions which allow them to be accepted into our great honor society.

The American Academy of Chefs was established in 1954 and has inducted more than 800 elite members into its honor rolls. *Your* induction ceremony will be held at the MGM Grand Hotel & Casino, Monday, July 22, 2002. (see tentative schedule of academy functions).

Thank you AAC! Joseph Amendola and Jon Greenwalt for sharing your knowledge in the culinary arts. And in memory to my food friend and fellow teacher, Alex Cline AAC, who has passed on.

Joseph Amendola passes away at age 87 January 23. 2008.

Joseph Amendola AAC
my Pastry Instructor
at CIA, Conn. 1960

Jon Greenwalt AAC
Capitol Chefs Assn.
AAC Hall of Fame 1990

Dear Mr. Volk,

Thank you for requesting information about the **Women Chefs & Restaurateurs (WCR)** association for your new book.

WCR is a dynamic organization dedicated to issues women face in the restaurant industry. In 1993 eight prominent chefs and restaurateurs *(Lidia Bastianich, Elka Gilmore, Joyce Goldstein, Johanne Killeen, Barbara Lazaroff, Mary Sue Milliken, Anne Rosenzweig and Barbara Tropp)* founded WCR to promote the education and advancement of women in the restaurant industry. In just 8 years, we have reached 2,000 members representing all sectors of the industry and still growing!

Thirteen cities across the US hold WCR events known as **WCR Exchange**. These events may be in the form of luncheons, speaking engagements, networking dinners, site tours, panel formats, etc. Each city has a Program Coordinator and is given flexibility in the type of event they hold. Lisa Hines, the National Coordinator, works with members that are interested in starting the WCR Exchange program in their city.

In the fall, we hold a **3-day Annual Conference** with Master Classes, Sunrise Seminars, Networking Champagne Receptions and fabulous culinary feasts prepared by our members. This year, we will be at the Loews Santa Monica Beach Hotel from October 27-29. Next year it will be Boston. We go from coast to coast each year.

Our new **Scholarship Program** has just closed for the 2001 year. This is our first year with 17 scholarship opportunities and we are very excited about the number and caliber of applicants. Included is the WCR Scholarship Brochure to give you an idea of what we offer our members.

WCR offers a wide range of benefits including: the Annual Membership Directory, a nationwide Job Bank, an Annual subscription to our quarterly newsletter *Entrez!*, and the monthly faxed WCR communiqué *Aperitif!*

If you have any additional questions, please feel free to call me at 1-877-927-7787.

Best regards,

Mary Beth Roth
Director of Member Services

The ACF. California Capital Chefs Association
Member Benefits

Post Office BOX 214171, Sacramento, California 95821

Active Culinary Membership qualifications include any person currently working in the culinary field of study that does wish to be classified as a Professional Chef, Cook, Pastry Chef, Pastry Apprentice, Cooks Apprentice, or Junior Member (in a Culinary or Pastry School Program).

The California Capital Chefs Association is one of the 240 Chapters that make up the American Culinary Federation.

All the amenities of The ACF found in the facts sheet are offered to all members of the CCCA, just for the asking. Additional benefits offered to the CCCA.

Leadership

Serving on the Board of Directors of your local chapter is an opportunity to both serve others and learn about how organizations are operated. The challenge of tackling a national office may be available to those who are ambitious.

Community Exposure

Working within your local chapter will give you a chance to earn the respect of your peers in the industry and the community in general. The events sponsored by the chapter are an opportunity to gain the attention of the local media and potential employers.

Achievement and Accreditation

- We can certify your credentials with our continual education opportunities.
- Stay current of industry changes.
- Local educational seminars and social meetings.
- Golf Tournaments.
- Culinary competition, opportunity to earn medals.
- Certification of your position held.
- Opportunity to train an apprentice.
- Opportunity to participate in local charity "Chef and Child" event.
- Participate in educational Regional Conference.
- Attend National ACF Conventions.
- Two thousand dollar life insurance coverage.
- Learn advanced leadership skills.
- Job referral services.
- Receive National Culinary Review.
- Center of Plate newsletter.
- The Academy of Chefs Honor Society.
- Local Chef of the Year Award, Junior member of the Year, Purveyor of the Year, Culinarian of the Year.
- Belonging to an organization of your colleagues can only enhance your future and professional standing within your profession.

This is to Certify

Adolph (Steve) Volk

ADOLPH M. VOLK

has been awarded

One of our Members, Steve Volk, C.P.C.
won the SILVER and BRONZE awards at the Worlds'
Fair held in Vancouver for his pastry presentations

Baked Foods Competition

Pacific Bakers Exhibition

B. C. Place

Awarded this 11 th day of August 1986

Official Judge:
....

Convention Chairman:
....

Committee Chairman:
....

★ ★

PACIFIC BAKERS EXHIBITION 1986
B.C. PLACE (the heart of EXPO 86)
Vancouver, British Columbia, Canada
August 11, 12, and 13, 1986

Adolph (Steve) Volk AAC World Culinary Olympics Award

Internationale Kochkunst-Ausstellung, Frankfurt, Germany
Awarded 1976 Culinary Olympic Gold Medal
Awarded 1984 Culinary Olympic Diploma of Honor
Awarded 1988 Culinary Olympic Culinary Excellence

UNITED STATES ARMY

THE QUARTERMASTER CORPS

January 9th, 1948

_____ Cpl Adolph H Volk, AA12 256 801 _____

has satisfactorily completed the Course of Instruction for

COURSE D--COOKS

Given at _____ Fort Sam Houston, Texas _____ this _____ ninth _____

day of _____ January _____ in the year _____ nineteen hundred forty-eight _____

_____ Troy E. Whiting
TROY C. WHITING
_____ ~~F. OGDEN,~~ Major, Quartermaster Corps
Asst ~~Gen~~ F. OGDEN, _Assistant Commandant._ _Commandant._
Capt., QC

UNITED STATES ARMY

THE QUARTERMASTER CORPS

September 2nd, 1949

SERGEANT ADOLPH M. VOLK, AF 12256801

has satisfactorily completed the Course of Instruction for

COURSE G--PASTRY BAKER

Given at THIRD ARMY AREA FOOD SERVICE SCHOOL, FORT BENNING, GEORGIA this SECOND

day of _____ SEPTEMBER _____ in the year _____ NINETEEN HUNDRED FORTY NINE _____

_____ Don le Romine
HARRY D. BASTIN DON C. ROMINE
CAPTAIN, QUARTERMASTER CORPS MAJOR., QUARTERMASTER CORPS
Assistant Commandant. _Commandant._

12

About the Author

ADOLPH (STEVE) VOLK, AAC
California Capitol Chefs Association
Chapter of the American Culinary Federation

PROFESSIONAL MEMBERSHIP

American Academy of Chefs (Honor Society)
Certified Executive Pastry Chef, ACF-CEPC (Life)
Certified Culinary Educator ACF   CCE
Retail Bakers of America-Master Baker   CMB
International Cake Exploration Societe & CA Chapter
1976 Culinary Olympics Gold Medal Winner, Germany

EDUCATION

West Valley College, Saratoga CA	Major Chefs Training
San Jose College, San Jose CA	Major Art Classes
Canada College, Redwood City CA	Major Food Service
University of California, Berkeley	Major Voc Ed Instructor
Sacramento State, Sacramento CA	Major Education & Art

CREDENTIALS

Culinary Arts Instructor (CA State License) Life
Bureau of Industrial Education, 1967 (Life) No. 3589 VTP
Standard Teaching Credential (Life) 1967, File 3786-90 kt
California Private Postsecondary Credential, No. 44159

SPECIAL CLASSES

Culinary Institute of America 1960, Air Force Culinary Scholarship
Statler Hilton, Waldorf Astoria & Governor Clinton Hotels - 1200 hours
Advance Hotel Training 1953-1955, New York & Chicago - 480 hours
1955 Research Formulas (major companies) Chicago - 320 hours
Quartermasters Chef 1948, Quartermasters Baker 1949, Military School

AWARDS
(While teaching)
1968-1988

Culinary Olympic Gold Medal, Germany 1976
Special Recognition, Culinary Olympics, Germany 1984 & 1988
Worlds Fair, Vancouver BC, Silver & Bronze Medals
McCormick Place Chicago (CA team) USA, 3rd place 1975

AWARDS
(While in AF)
1950-1962

Geneva Culinaire & Pan American Awards 1962
Societe Culinaire Philanthropique, New York - France
Won national & international awards 1952-1961
Air Force (individual) culinary trophy 1960
World Food Conference 1959, PA. Total 10 awards
United Nations Award, silver, 1958, NY. Total 6 awards

SPECIAL ASSIGNMENTS

Exec. Pastry Chef, Ice Carvings, Catering, Cake Decorator
Pres. Harry S. Truman, 1948, Kirtland AFB, Albequerque NM
Pres. Dwight D. Eisenhower, 1955, Opening of AF Academy, Denver CO
Pres. John F. Kennedy, 1962, Egland AFB, Ft. Walton Beach FL
VP Lyndon Johnson, 1962, Egland AFB & Washington DC
Headquarters Alaska Air Command (Chateau) Anchorage AK
Bob Hope w/TV & Hollywood All Star Troops, USO events

MILITARY SERVICE

US Navy 1942-1946
US Air Force 1946-1962
Disabled Veteran

Retired
100% disability

His Eminence Cardinal Spellman, Kruchev of Russia1, Mary Martin, Marilyn Monroe, Jane Mansfield, Dean Martin, Sammy Davis, Jr., Jerry Lewis, etc. Headquarters Continental Air Command, Mitchel Field NY & United Nations NY. Princess Grace of Monaco as well as other known personalities. *As pastry chef, I had the privilege of meeting and serving the names above.*

Volk's start in baking came, of all places in the Air Force Baking School. He served in that branch of the service until his retirement. He also got training with the major restaurant chains at the Waldorf Astoria, Statler Hilton and Governor Clinton Hotels in New York City

Added to that, have been special studies with several noted European chefs.

Being awarded this trophy for an event which I have forgotten. I call it "old timers".

14

Alex and I both graduated 9/11/67 from UC Berkeley upon completion of two years training in Vocationa Education with a life time credential for grades 9 through 14.

greatest of
gifts
are family
and
friends.

Alex Cline was my supervisor at Canada College in Culinary Arts.

To An
Honored
Friend

Alec Cline

עוֹלָם
אֵל אֶחָד
וּבָּעָ יִשָּׁר

After completing my assignment at Mitchel Air Force Base in Long Island NY I was reassigned to the Headquarters Pentagon Washington DC. under the command of General Curtis Lemay. Upon arriving there I was asked if I would be interested in going with 85 other NCO's to open the first Air Force Academy in Denver CO. Being at high altitude, food preparation would be different than at a lower altitude. Due to this I was sent to school in Chicago to learn about the physics and chemistry of baking at a high altitude. This knowledge proved to be valuable to the Air Force food service program and of course to the cadets at the Air Force Academy at which I remained for two years.

Cake for Pres. Dwight D. Eisenhower and other VIP's (1955)
Opening of the Air Force Academy, Lowery AFB, Denver CO

Cake design taken from blueprints of the Academy in Colorado Springs CO. Letter on cake from Pres. Dwight D. Eisenhower.

PRESIDENTIAL CAKE -- TSgt. Adolph "Steve" Volk of the Central Pastry Kitchen puts the finishing touches on his third cake for a President during almost 20 years of military service. TSgt. Volk, Executive Pastry Chef (R.B.A. Master Baker) has make cakes for Presidents Truman, Eisenhower and Kennedy. This beauty rounds out his career as he has tentative plans to retire at the end of this year.
   • US Navy 1942-46 (38 months) South Pacific • US Air Force 1946-1962 (Ret.)

It was a great honor to have served by decorating cakes and sculpting ice for so many dignitaries as well as providing cakes and ice sculptures for dining halls, NCO clubs, officers clubs and at the Chateau in Alaska. The VIP's were many, from heads of government, foreign and US, religious dignitaries and Hollywood stars who entertained the GI's. It was during a fire power missile demonstration that I was asked to decorate the above cake and to be on the greeting staff.

Upon entering the officer's club greeting area, I had the privilege to shake hands with Pres. Kennedy, Vice Pres. Johnson and General Lemay. I stood next to Johnson for the next five hours. On this occasion we were ordered to guard the social events. We were in full dress uniform, along with the FBI

THE WORLDS LARGEST REVOLVING CAKE
by Adolph M. (Steve) Volk

In May of 1975, Dr. Devins, Dean of Education in Food Service and two well dressed gentlemen from Canada walked into the start of my three hour baking class at West Valley College (Saratoga Campus). They wanted to see me in private. The students, 32 in all, had their assignments and knew what they had to do.

We sat down in the school dining room . I was told that three areas in the United States were selected to do a worlds highest, 32 foot, decorated cake in celebration of the 200th birthday of America. This was a non-profit project with donated labor. It was financed thru a bank in Canada and Japan to pay all other expenses. The estimate of the amount of fruit cake was over 20 tons. This was to revolve for about 45 days indoors, from mid November 1945 to January 2, 1976, under the rotunda at the Emporium in San Francisco.

The motors and center steel post would be part of the platform to house the fruit cake. There were 18 panels to be iced, with art work depicting the history of California. Three flat railroad motors were used to rotate the cake. The men wanted to know whether or not I would undertake this project and accept the challenge. They were then flying to New York and Boston where they were looking for other volunteers to tackle a like project at those locations. I later found out that noone wanted the task. Still overwhelmed, I was asked to join the team. Dr. Devins felt confident I could do it. Up to that time, the tallest cake I did was an 11 foot wedding cake for the New York Culinary Art Show.

I returned to the classroom and told the students what had transpired. Their response was to "Go for It!". I then went to Dr. Devins office where the staff were having coffee and sandwiches and announced that I would do it.

I purchased light panel marine plywood for all weather conditions, having the plywood cut into panels to go on the outside of the fruit cake. Next I stretched and stapled chicken wire over the plywood for first coat of royal icing. The second coat of icing was for the art work done by Steve and Sharon Volk, with the information done on 3x5 butcher paper. Using a 20 qt. mixing bowl with 12 lbs. of C&H sugar, 8 oz. Westco Deco Whip, (meringue powder) 1/2 oz. cream of tarter, sifting twice, added 8 oz. white vinegar to aid colors, 12 oz. glucose to prevent cracks, with 1 1/2 to 2 pints of water.

The panels were taken to the Emporium. At this point we had much help from the students from West Valley and Canada College food service training programs. The panels were put into place with strips of vee shaped metal to hold them together.

The cake was baked in tunnel ovens by a bakery in L.A. I believe the name was Thee's. A five foot bird (which we constructed) called a Phoenix was placed on the cake. This bird supposedly rose from the 1906 earthquake. At this point the cake was 37 feet tall.

Two tons of cake was donated to charity to feed the hungry at Thanksgiving. Cut from the inside, thru a trap door at the base of the cake . Another two tons at Christmas. The remainder was sold in three pound boxes to cover the cost of materials. All monies exceeding the cost was donated to charities.

THE WORLDS LARGEST REVOLVING CAKE

San Francisco Bicentennial Birthday Cake 1776 * 1976
Created and Design by Creative Cake by Volk in Saratoga, CA
Description: 18 Icing panels, 32 feet tall, 40,000 pounds, a 5-foot Phoenix Bird rising out of the San Francisco Fire (37 ft).

Bicentennial cake displayed at the San Francisco Emporium from mid November 1975 to January 2, 1976.

The most famous example of Volk's talent could be the 32 foot masterpiece he created for San Francisco's Bicentennial celebration. The three tiered, six sided cake featured 18 gigantic panels, depicting well known events in the city's history - easy stuff, like detailing Francis Drakes discovery of San Francisco, the 1906 earthquake and fire, the construction of the Golden Gate Bridge, the Cliff House and the Palace of Fine Arts in icing. In other words, the fact the cake was 32 feet tall wasn't enough of a challenge. Nor was revolving the cake; requiring three motors, and perfect balance of 32 feet of cake and frosting in a city known for its fault line. Throw in 18 panels of art and 200 "candles" made of airplane lights covered in frosting, and it may give you an idea of where this mans brilliance can lead you.

Four tons of cake was donated to charity at Thanksgiving and Christmas. All monies exceeding expenses was donated. All work and labor donated as a community activity.

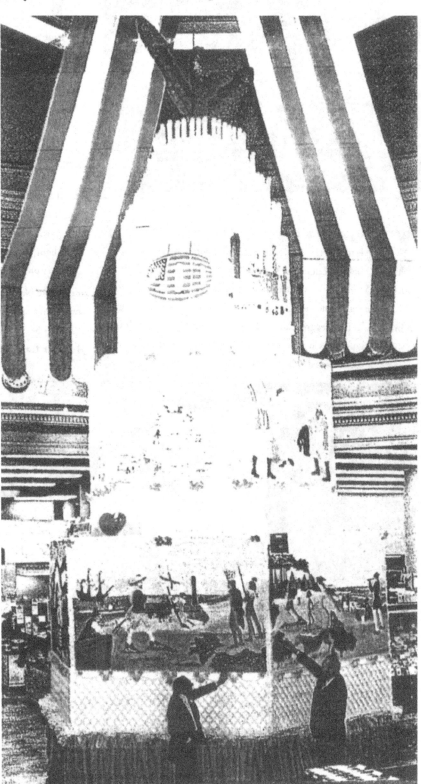

School of Creative Cakes   *By Volk*

The Baking Education Center, Bakery and Baker's Store at King Arthur Flour are located off Interstate 91 in Norwich, Vermont. If you're planning an extended visit or your next vacation, there's much to do in the area – we're located just across the river from Hanover, New Hampshire, home of Dartmouth College, and are only minutes from the picturesque villages of Quechee and Woodstock, Vermont. We're a comfortable drive from Boston, Hartford and New York, and there's a wide range of lodging choices available nearl information, or assistance in finding accommodation 800.652.3334, or visit our Web site: www.KingArtht

Directions

From the South: Take I-91 North to exit 13. Follow ramp, turn left at the light and go under the highway next light, turn left onto Route 5 South. We're the se business on the left, less than 1/2 mile from the light.

From the North: Take I-91 South to exit 13. Follow ramp, and at the light go straight through the interse Route 5 South. We're the second business on the left, 1/2 mile from the light.

Do you love to bake, or have you always wanted to learn? If the answer is "yes," we invite you to visit the Baking Education Center at King Arthur Flour in Norwich, Vermont. Passionate bakers and bread connoisseurs will plunge into hands-on courses at our school, taste a sampling of breads and pastries from our bakery, and shop for hard-to-find tools and ingredients at our retail store – a destination where your every baking need will be satisfied.

Certified Master Baker Jeffrey Hamelman (right) teaches professional-level courses at the Center.

The Baker's Catalogue, Inc.
133 Route 5 South
Post Office Box 876
Norwich, Vermont 05055-0876
800.652.3334
www.KingArthurFlour.com

Fourth Senior Olympics of Practical Cookery · San Francisco 1970

The National Restaurant Association The Golden Gate Restaurant Association and The Chefs' Association of the Pacific Coast

Extend their sincerest appreciation for your valuable contribution as participant in the 5th Western National Restaurant Convention Senior Practical Culinary Olympics

presented to:

Adolph Volk

September 1970   San Francisco

Robert Jensen   *Dan A. Brenda*

Convention General Chairman   President
     Jean Joaquin Golden Gate Restaurant
     Chairman   Association
     Culinary Arts

American Culinary Federation

Educational Institute

Adolph M. Volk

Has qualified by training and experience to be certified
by the rules and standards of the American Culinary Federation
as a

Certified Executive Pastry Chef

American Culinary Federation

Educational Institute

Adolph M. Volk

Has qualified by training and experience to be certified
by the rules and standards of the American Culinary Federation
as a

Certified Culinary Educator

Life

Adolph (Steve) Volk—Master Baker

Published, Sacramento Bee

By Nancy Mandelbert

When hosting dinner for heads of state, or a party of four to 4,000 of your closest friends, by all means, don't forget the dessert. This especially holds true if your event calls for something spectacular. Let's say a company is commemorating a new building and the occasion begs the distinctive touch; such as a 30-foot, towering replica in cake and icing. Perhaps you would like special effects; a waterfall, a few fountains, Star Wars in frosting? Whether you are a restaurateur, a meeting planner, or the mother of the bride, finding the talent and creativity you need for a special occasion isn't always a cakewalk through the Yellow Pages. If your event could put outstanding talent and creativity to good use, my recommendation is to check out Volk's Cake and Cooky Company.

Throughout his 57 year career. Steve Volk's baking accomplishments have amazed, astonished, and boggled the mind, earning respect and honors from the highest levels. Yet, he credits "inspiration" and the military for making him what he is today. Nicknamed "the Rembrandt of Pastry," "Doctor Dough," and "the George Lukas of Dessert," the man is indeed a master. His works exemplify his artistry, imagination and sense of humor, throughout his impressive career of making the impossible a reality with a "spoonful of sugar."

The most famous example of Volk's talent could be the 32-foot masterpiece he created for San Francisco's Bicentennial celebration. The three-tiered, six-sided cake featured 18 gigantic panels, depicting well-known events in the city's history—easy stuff, like detailing Francis Drake's discovery of San Francisco, the 1906 earthquake and fire, the construction of the Golden Gate Bridge, the Cliff House and the Palace of Fine Arts in icing. In other words, the fact the cake was 32 feet tall wasn't enough of a challenge. Nor was revolving the cake; requiring three motors, and perfect balance of 32 feet of cake and frosting in a city known for its fault line. Throw in 18 panels of art and 200 "candles" made of airplane lights covered in frosting, and it may give you an idea of where this man's brilliance can lead you.

Remember the fabulous pastries at Carmel's Highland's Inn? Steve Volk was the executive pastry chef there in the early Eighties. Before that, Volk was chosen to bake for notables like Truman, Eisenhower, Kennedy, and LBJ, Bob Hope, Marilyn Monroe, Jayne Mansfield (guess what he recreated on their cakes), Mary Martin, Dean Martin, Jerry Lewis, Sammy Davis, Cardinal Spellman, Kruschev, and Princess Grace of Monaco. If you think the above list is a simple matter of being in the right place at the right time, let's add a little recognition to make our plaudits credible. No state fair contests for this guy. Volk's accomplishments have earned national and worldwide respect. An impressive list of competitions, including the World Culinary Olympics, Salon of Culinary Arts, Geneva Culinaire and Pan Am awards; just to name a few.

Ironically, for all his accomplishments, Steve Volk is a bit of an understatement. Diminutive in size, but gigantic in the talent contained within, his bakery sits, almost unnoticeable, in a small shopping center on the corner of Sunrise and Madison. A mere press of the nose against the bakery's front window lends little enlightenment as to what can be found inside. Rows of tin cake pans in various sizes and shapes hang from the ceiling. Wedding cake samples grace an efficient but cramped storefront. A glass counter filled with fresh pastries of every description runs the length of one wall, leaving a narrow space for customers and seating, which is somewhat ironic considering the indulgences of the wares purveyed within.

Once inside, the real story begins to reveal itself in the form of plaques, awards, news articles and letters commending television appearances, hanging on the wall. The wall also bears photos of some of his work; monuments to showboats and ships, New York's skyline, the Taj Mahal, Seattle's Space Needle, and the Arc Di Triomphe (under which a couple was married). Each photo shows Volk bearing a broad grin, looking rightfully proud. Maybe that's the secret of Volk's success; a genuine love for what he does.

SEVENTEENTH ANNUAL

Pan American

HOTEL & RESTAURANT
EXPOSITION

MIAMI'S DOWNTOWN BAYFRONT AUDITORIUM

OCTOBER 23, 24, 25, 1962

This is to certify that

T/SGT. ADOLPH M. VOLK

of the..........**EGLIN AIR FORCE BASE**..........

has been awarded this certificate in recognition of
an outstanding demonstration while participating
in the *first live demonstration* officially known as
"Master Chefs On Stage."

In *Testimony whereof,* we hereunto subscribed our
names and caused the seal of the Pan American
Hotel & Restaurant Exposition *to be affixed hereto*
by its duly authorized officers this..........**25**..........
day of..........**OCTOBER**.........., 1962.

James J Maske
President

Lillian C. Claughton.
Vice President

Harry L Hoffman
Chairman

24

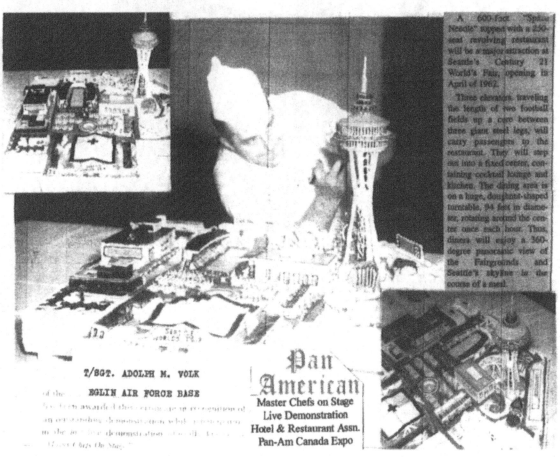

A 600-foot "Space Needle" topped with a 250-seat revolving restaurant will be a major attraction at Seattle's Century 21 World's Fair, opening in April of 1962.

Three elevators, traveling the length of two football fields up a core between three giant steel legs, will carry passengers to the restaurant. They will step out into a fixed center, containing cocktail lounge and kitchen. The dining area is on a huge, doughnut-shaped turntable, 94 feet in diameter, rotating around the center once each hour. Thus, diners will enjoy a 360-degree panoramic view of the Fairgrounds and Seattle's skyline in the course of a meal.

T/SGT. ADOLPH M. VOLK
of the EGLIN AIR FORCE BASE

Pan American
Master Chefs on Stage
Live Demonstration
Hotel & Restaurant Assn.
Pan-Am Canada Expo

OFFICE OF INFORMATION, ACCEPTS AWARD FOR TSGT ADOLPH M. VOLK, JR., 3201ST SUPPORT SQUADRON, EGLIN AIR FORCE BASE, FLORIDA, PRESENTED BY THE SOCIETE CULINAIRE PHILANTHROPIQUE, NEW YORK CITY. T/SGT VOLK WON FIRST PRIZE FOR SUGAR WORK AND ORIGINALITY AT THE 93RD ANNUAL SALON OF CULINARY ART AT THE NEW YORK COLISEUM, NOVEMBER 1961.

Master Chef Volk's Winning
Cakes Pretty As A Picture

1st PRIZE for ORIGINALITY

CULINARY ARTS AWARD - - Col. Ronald F. Fellows, Base Commander, presents the first place award for Sugar Work and Originality from the Societe Culinaire Philanthropique to SSgt. Adolph M. Volk, Jr., whose entry in the 93rd Annual Salon of Culinary Art won him this honor. Volk, with the 3201st Support Squadron, has more than twenty other awards received in competition.

Hands on hotel training in Europe. While in the military I also had this training in baking and cooking. Check with your culinary school for an extern-ship or with the American Academy of Chefs (ACF). 1-800-624-9458

Eight Week Advance Hotel Training Course At;

Hotel: Statler and the Hotel Governor Clinton
Waldorf- Astoria, New York City 24 weeks training

Statler-Hilton Hotel Training.........................Training 8 weeks, 384 hours
Waldorf-Astoria Hotel Training.....................Training 8 weeks, 416 hours
Governor Clinton Hotel Training...................Training 8 weeks, 400 hours
                                                                    A Total of 1200 hours ·

Mitchel Air Force Base, New York

Staff Sergeant Adolph M. Volk, Jr.
AF 12256801
5040th Support Group
Elmendorf Air Force Base, Alaska

FRANK A. ARMSTRONG, JR.
Lieutenant General, USAF
Commander in Chief

Culinary Institute of America, New Haven, Connecticut.
Advance Baking Class (1960) with Joseph Amendola, Instructor.

Melvin

Wulser

Steve Volk

Instructor Amendola

Hans

Academy of Chefs Dinner
Joseph Amendola
Steve Volk (standing)
Jon Greenwalt

The Culinary Institute of America   Baking & Pastry

The Vocational Education Department
of CSP Sacramento
presents this

Certificate of Appreciation

to

ADOLPH VOLK

For your valuable contribution to the
California State Prison Sacramento
Vocational Programs
Trade Advisory Committee

Supervisor of Vocational
Instruction

Warden

Supervisor of Correctional
Education Programs

Eagles are the most long-lived bird in the world. By the time they reach 40 years old, their claws will start to age, losing their effectiveness and making it hard for them to catch preys. The lifespan of an eagle is up to 70 years old. But in order to live this long, it must make the toughest decision at 40. At 40, its beak is too long and curvy that it reaches its chest. Its wings, full of long, thickened feathers, are too heavy for easy flying. The eagle is left with 2 choices – do nothing and await its death or go through a painful period of transformation and renewal.

For 150 days, it first trains itself to fly beyond the high mountains, build and live in its nest and cease all flying activities. It then begins to knock its beak against granite rocks till the beak is completely removed. When a new beak is grown, the eagle will use it to remove all its old claws and await quietly for new ones to be fully grown. When the new claws are fully grown, the eagle will use them to remove all its feathers, one by one. Five months later, when its new feathers are fully grown, it will soar in the sky again with renewed strength and is able to live for the next 30 years.

In life, as an individual, in a ministry, even in an organization, sometimes, we have to learn to make difficult decisions so as to make room for changes. Changes bring about renewal. And the only way for us to soar again is to let go old ways, old habits, old lives. For as long as we are prepared to put aside our old baggage - past glory or shame, past success or failure - be willing to become zero, with an empty cup mentality, we will be able to discover our potential and head towards a renewed perspective in any aspect of our lives.

Lt. Col. Frank H. Martin
Commander
3201st Support Squadron
Eglin AFB, Florida

Dear Sir:

I would like to bring to your attention the outstanding service one of your men, T/Sgt. Adolph M. Volk, has rendered to the Boy Scout Program.

I feel that Boy Scouting has the best program for developing the youth of our nation of any of the youth movements. The Choctawhatchee District is providing this program for slightly less than 2,000 boys. In order for this program to be successful, continue to expand and serve, it takes leadership and men such as T/Sgt. Volk who are willing and able to give freely of their time and talents.

T/Sgt. Volk is certainly a credit to the Air Force. It is through the individual efforts of such men as this that keeps the Air Force-Community relationship on such a high plane. Each of us could well take a lesson from this fine man in service to others.

I'm sure that each of the individual Boy Scout Units which have received help from T/Sgt. Volk would join the Choctawhatchee District in commending him for a job well done.

Yours for Better Scouting,

Eli F. Sapp, Jr.
Chairman
Choctawhatchee District, B. S. A.

TO: TSgt Adolph M. Volk
3201st Support Squadron
Eglin AFB, Fla.

1. It gives me great pleasure to forward the attached letter of appreciation from Mr. Eli F. Sapp, Jr., Chairman, Choctawhatchee District, Boy Scouts of America.

2. Your unselfish efforts in furtherance of the aims of Boy Scouting is commendable. We all share in the good will generated by the recognition of your endeavors in the local community.

FRANK H. MARTIN
LT COL, USAF
Commander

1 Atch
Ltr fr Mr Sapp

Culinary Art Awards
New York
1953/1954/1957
1958/1959/1961

Ice Carving Awards
←-1955 and 1958-→
First Place Award

ADOLPH (STEVE) VOLK, (US Air Force)

Salon of Culinary Arts, NY·1958 (1st place)

Société Culinaire Philanthropique
de New York, Inc.

ANNUAL SALON of CULINARY ART

33

S A C R A M E N T O   C O U N·T Y   O F F I C E   O F   E D U C A T I O N

9738 LINCOLN VILLAGE DRIVE • SACRAMENTO, CALIFORNIA 95827 • (916) 366-2591

Mr. Adolph M. Steve Volk
5115 Rimwood Dr.
Fair Oaks, CA 95628

DAVID P. MEANEY, Ed.D.
Superintendent
(916) 366-2593

Dear STEVE VOLK

Your assistance is needed in evaluating and improving school programs aimed at training students for employment in your industry. We would appreciate your cooperation in completing the attached survey which is designed to help us determine which skills you require of beginning (entry-level) employees.

The survey contains skills taught in Sacramento area schools as well as skills from other sources. We would like to know which skills you require for the specific occupation listed at the top of the survey. The last page provides space for any comments you wish to add.

Your contribution to Vocational Education planning and evaluation is valuable to the schools and the students. We hope you will benefit also, as people with qualifications better suited to your needs become available in the job market. We know the demands on your time are already great, but we would appreciate it if you would complete the survey and return it as soon as possible. If you have any questions regarding the survey, please contact the Vocational Education Department at (916) 366-2581.

We at the County Office of Education thank you for your cooperation and your time in completing the enclosed survey.

Sincerely,

David P. Meaney
County Superintendent

34

ROP Bakery Academy Program

&

ROP Restaurant & Commercial Food Preparation Program

Presents This

Certificate of Appreciation

to

Steve Volk
Volk's Cake & Cooky

for 8 years of dedicated service as a member of the Advisory Committee Council
and making these ROP Programs one of the finest job training programs in the
State of California
Presented this 8th day of February, 2001

Carol Ference
Carol Ference, SJUSD, ROP Coordinator

Sally A Edwards
Sally A. Edwards, Instructor BakeryAcademy

Sandi Coulter
Sandi Coulter, Instructor Restaurant & Commercial Food

For Eight Years

California Association FHA-HERO
Certificate of Appreciation

PRESENTED TO

STEVE VOLK

*In Recognition of Special Services to the Regional
Educational Activities and Instructional Programs of the
Future Homemakers of America –
Home Economics Related Occupations*

Paula Tripp
Region Advisor

January 29, 2000

Date

Jack Fry
Region President

Basic Cake Decorating Classes

Student's Name _____ Date_____

Home Phone # _____ Work Phone # _____

INTRODUCTION • CLASS SAFETY & SANITATION • ITS PURPOSE
• INFORMATION AND FEEDBACK IN CLASS

☐ Demo — Folding a Paper Cone -- Its Purpose -- Using Large and Small Cones -- Pastry Bag

☐ Demo — *Splitting, Reverse and Filling a Cake -- Crumb Coating & Icing a Cake*

☐ Demo — How to Use our Kopy Kake -- Outline Drawings on Cakes

☐ Demo — How to use Silk Screens with Air Spray to Decorate Cakes

☐ Demo — Using the Air Spray for Background and Coloring -- In Art Work on Cakes

☐ Demo — Drawings and Ideas for Holiday Art -- When to Find & Purchase Ideas

☐ Demo — Borders, Shell, Reverse, Rope, Garland, Triple Reverse

☐ Demo — Piping, Clowns, Elephants, Balloons, Cornelli and Writing

☐ Demo — *Sweet Peas, Half Roses, Half Carnations, Half Roses & Buds*

☐ Demo — Full Roses (1-3-5), American Roses, Pine Cone Roses

HANDS-ON — In the time remaining, pick up the tubes and practice.

We supply the icing and boards to practice with in class.
We will also provide items needed for Class, for Hands-on, and Practice

Coffee and cake will be served in class during feedback at Lunch time.

Included in your class fee are the following:

Decorating tubes #3, #12, #16, #22, #104 and #125 — Pastry Bags (1) each - #12 and #14, with two (2) couplers

FREE "Maid of Scandinavia" catalog (to order from) — FREE Recipes and handouts

Bring from Home: Scissors, washcloth, towels and apron

- Materials, Tools and Classroom Fee (Paid in Advance)
- Classes are open with the first six students to sign up (PAID IN FULL)
- Eight students per class maximum, allowing for two if late sign-up
- Classes begin on_____morning at 9:00 AM sharp -- Date: _____
- ½ hour lunch break around noon, classes will be completed by 3:30 PM (6-hour Training)

Unemployed, Low Paying Job Books By Adolph Steve Volk Cost Less, Thru AuthorHouse 1-888-519-5121 - (Ext. 5023)

Classes for beginners, home use, the hobbyist, and just for fun! **AutherHouse Bookstore**

Basic Gingerbread House Classes for beginners, home use, the hobbyist, recreation, and just for fun!

Student's Name_____ Date_____

Home Phone # _____ Work Phone # _____

To save time and for better results, your GINGERBREAD HOUSE has been pre-mixed, refrigerated, rolled out prebaked, cut out, <u>assembled, and placed on our board</u> . . . saving your hours of work, refrigeration time and baking time.

In class you will receive information on all the above, including recipes to follow later to use at home, everything from Gingerbread dough, icing and patterns. You can have a life time of fun, during the holiday season making Gingerbread houses for your friends as a gift, teach your children or grandchildren to make Gingerbread house.

Royal Icing is provided in class for decorating as well as other items such as candies, pretzels, gum drops M&M's, candy canes, ice cream cones for trees, meringue snowmen, piping gel for ice pond, clinging powdered sugar for snow and much more.

You may wish to bring a camera to class to photograph your art work as well as your fellow students and their completed art work on the Gingerbread houses.

- Gingerbread dough   • Ingredients   • Mixing   • Baking   • Set Up   • W/Instructions

- Tuff Boardi for Houses and Decorations   • Photos & Drawings for New Ideas   • Recipes

Lab Fee: _____

- Bring from Home: Scissors, washcloth, towels, apron.

WOUNDED WARRIOR PROJECT®

Classroom Fee: _____

- Classes are open with the first six students to sign up (PAID IN FULL)
- Eight students per class maximum, allowing for two if late sign-up
- Classes begin on Monday morning at 9:00 AM sharp - Date: _____
- ½ hour lunch break around noon, classes will be completed by 3:30 PM (6-hour Training)

Total Fee: _____

Some of our Culinary College & Baker Hand Craft Students will wrap some of their gingerbread houses & cookies in saran wrap to take to Children's and Veterans Hospitals, also for the very poor. Also you can buy the gingerbread house kit in stores, for someone who is in need of recreation due to being handicapped as a fun gift.

T/Sgt Adolph (Steve) Volk /ncoic/exec chef & pastery chef at the officers club (gold room) Mitchal air force base, Air Command Center, Long Island N.Y. in (1960) the base closed 50 years ago (WOW) time flies when you enjoy your type of work,and I did Yes I miss catering parties,doing ice carvings,& special events

Salon of Culinary Arts, NY 1955-1958. 1st place

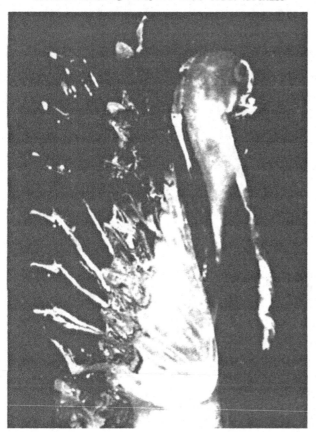
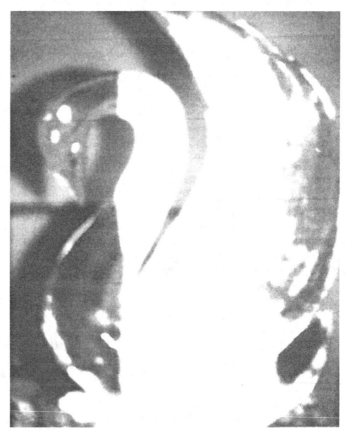

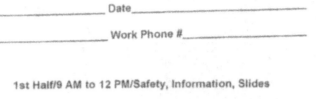

Basic Ice Carving Classes   FREE

Student's Name_____ Date_____

Home Phone #_____ Work Phone #_____

Alva & Steve Volk
Owners/Management

Membership (1989) National Ice Craving
Association 1st Award (1955) Ice Carving
Culinary Art Salon - New York City, N.Y.

1st Half/9 AM to 12 PM/Safety, Information, Slides

- □ Safety - What to wear, clothing, gloves, safety glasses
- □ Safety - Sharpness of tools, danger of chain saw
- □ Safety - Keep hands clear of partner's tools in use
- □ Safety - Keep area clean of broken ice. Sweep clean.
- □ How to order your ice, types of ice, transportation of ice
- □ Carving inside freezer and why, carving outside is alright
- □ Carving in hotels, country clubs, ships, catering, freelance
- □ Storing ice carving, delivery, set ups and draining trays

Slide Presentation

- □ Students first time, West Valley and Canada College
- □ Students first time, (S.E.T.A.) Bakers Hand Craft School
- □ Students second time, Private School, Pacific Coast College
- □ U.S. teams and Canada teams, ice carvings in Chicago

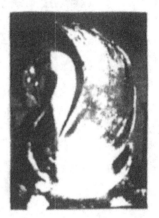

Air Force Academy

2nd Half/12:30 PM to 3:30 PM

- □ Blocks of ice due around 12 PM, setting ice in place
- □ Set tools out - return, when not in use for safety
- □ Ask for help, when you need it, will advise you, what to do
- □ Watch for cracks or hollow sounds in the ice, work another area
- □ Bring your camera, to have your photo, with your ice craving

They had a design on paper and put the template on the ice, chipping along the outline with a pronged pick. We can see the girls using the pronged picks to chip away extra ice. In this way they get used to the ice and the sounds, listening for cracks. Later they will use hand saws to cut away large amounts of ice. The pronged pick is the same tool as the "chipper chopper", often used to cut blocks of chocolate.

Litchel Field & United Nations

Cost of (Average) Block of Ice and Delivery - $54.00
#2 - Two Students on Block of Ice - $27.00 Extra Ea.
#3 - Three Students on Block of Ice - $18.00 Extra Ea.

Lab Fee
Classroom Fee   **FREE**
Cost of Ice Block   _____
Total   _____

□ #2 - Two Students Per Ice Block
Classroom Fee
　　Lab Fee   **FREE**
Cost of Ice Block $27.00 Extra

□ #3 - Three Students Per Ice Block
Classroom Fee
　　Lab Fee   **FREE**
Cost of Ice Block $18.00 Extra

Second (or) More Times in (Our) Ice Carving Class.
./ Just show up for the 2nd half.

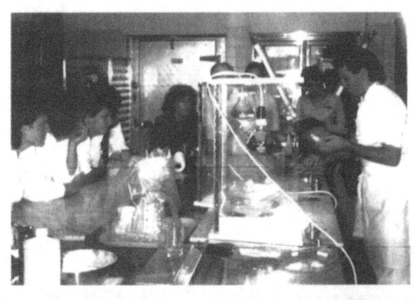

If you have interest in
learning step by step of
pulled @ blowen sugar,
recipes @ equipment
go to the book below
Culinary Olympics
cost $29.00 plus s/h
thru Auther House
1-(888)-519-5121

400 Color Photos

Part One.. 1 thru 14
    Volks Cake & Cooky Co. (cakes)
    Education Info-Skill Centers & Jr. Colleges
    Professional Schools & related info
    Classes recommended by ACF/RBA/NRA
    Assn. for Wedding Professional International
    (WACS) World Assn. of Cooks Societies
Part Two...... .... 15 thru 35
    Pulled & blown sugar with recipies
    Step b6 step rose & swan by Pastry Wiz.com
    Classes taken with Peter Boyle
    Classes taken with Ewald Notter
Part Three..35 thru 53
    Culinary Olympics sugar displays
        1976/1984/1988
Part Four..54 thru 62
    US chefs preparing food displays
    In honor of Chef Gerhard Grimeissen 2/26/95
    World Wide Culinary Students under 23 years
    Culinary Olympic Judges keeping daily scores
Part Five............ .... 63 thru 74
    Food trays prepared & designed by chefs
    Sheraton Hotel's 1976 Art Displays
Part Six................. ....75 thru 95
    Culinary Olympics assorted displays
Part Seven ....95 thru 115
    Culinary Olympics assorted displays
    Final pages of Gingerbread Houses

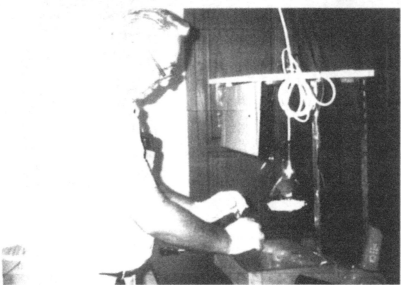

Basic Cake Decorating #1
12 Weeks   7-10 p.m.
One Night Per Week

(Fall or Spring) Semester
With Steve Volk A.C.F.
R.B.A. Master, C.E.P.C./C.C.E.

Introduction to Cake Decorating

1. Roll Call & Introduction
2. Safety & Sanitation
3. Orientation & Objectives
4. Recipes & Information Handouts
5. Tools & Equipment Needed

Learning Control of Tools & Icing

1. Set Up Pastry Bags & Tubes
2. Folding Paper Cones & Uses
3. Piping Stars, Curves & Lines
4. Proper Control, with Quality
5. Shell, Reverse & Rope Borders

Borders with Quality

1. Review Shell, Reverse & Rope Borders
2. Triple Reverse, Inside Borders
3. Eliptical Shell Borders
4. Learn Speed, Control with Quality
5. Basket Weave Construction

Figure Piping in Icing

1. (3-D) Figure (B.C.) Piping
2. Demo Projects, Review Books
3. Piping Clowns & Elephants
4. Demo Piping Gel Balloons
5. Practice Piping, More Figures

Piping Gel (Agar) Art Work

1. (Demo) Proper Colors, Dual & Icing
2. (Demo) Piping Gel Transfer
3. Kopy Kake and Art (Information)
4. Silk Screen & Air Gun (Information)
5. Your Project, Piping Gel Transfer

Piping Gel Transfers & Backgrounds

1. Icing on Cardboard or Styrofoam
2. Combing in Background with Colors
3. Sky, Water, Sunset, Hills & Beaches
4. Tracing Paper, Transfers from Last Week
5. Placing Borders with Art Work

Half Way Mark (Special)

1. Bring a Friend & Popcorn
2. Past Students, Project (Slides)
3. Culinary Olympics Germany (Slides)
4. Break, Feedback & Hand Outs
5. Best of All, Calif. & ICERs (Slides)

Introduction to Icing Flowers

1. Demo with Hands-On Following
2. (Three Types) of Icing Sweet Peas
3. Rose Buds (Closed & Open) 2/3
4. Half Roses & Half Carnations
5. Stems, Leaves & Bows

Introduction to Full Roses

1. Special Roses, Dual Colors
2. Center & Reverse on Flower Nail
3. Add Three/To Petals Base
4. Add (5) Long, Then (7) Short
5. Tea Rose (4 & 4), Pine Cone (21)

Additional Buttercream Flowers

1. Assorted Spring Blossoms
2. Mums, Daffodils, Pansies
3. Daisies, Poinsettia, Mini Pine Cones
4. Lily of the Valley
5. Cabbage Rose

How to Set Up Wedding Cakes

1. Wedding Cake Separators & Fountains
2. Pining & Stacking Wedding Cake
3. Extra Borders (Side) & Cannilli
4. Vine Clusters & Side Sweet Peas
5. Delivery & Expectations

Decorating Your Cake (Finals)

1. Bring in Your (Pre-Iced) Cake
2. Use Your Idea or One of Mine
3. Add on Borders, Writing & Flowers
4. Open for Piping, Transfer & Art
5. Show & Tell, Any One for Cake?

CITATION TO ACCOMPANY THE AWARD OF

THE AIR FORCE COMMENDATION MEDAL

TO

ADOLPH M. VOLK

Staff Sergeant Adolph M. Volk, AF 12 256 801, distinguished himself by meritorious achievement during the period 1 August 1958 to 1 January 1959, while serving as Noncommissioned Officer-in-Charge of the Bread Bakery, 5040th Support Group, Elmendorf Air Force Base, Alaska. On 20 August 1958, Sergeant Volk was sent to Eielson Air Force Base to provide greatly needed technical assistance and training for personnel of the bread bakery. Within a very short time, he improved the quality of the bread and increased production which eliminated exhorbitant waste and made good quality bread available. Sergeant Volk represented Elmendorf Air Force Base and the Air Force in the Salon of Culinary Art held at the National Hotel Exposition in New York City from 3 to 7 November 1958. He competed against the leading civilian chefs of the United States and twenty-seven other countries and won a total of ten top awards. By his initiative, superior culinary knowledge, and ingenuity, Sergeant Volk has brought credit upon himself, the Alaskan Air Command, and the United States Air Force.

FRANK A. ARMSTRONG, JR.
Lieutenant General, USAF
Commander in Chief

These two photos are of my first class at West Valley College. Starting with the art of mixing, testing and baking assorted breads.

I started teaching the art of baking in 1966 at West Valley College, at the Campbell campus, CA. 20 students attended as part of the restaurant training program, I then moved to the new campus at Saratoga CA, teaching four classes with 24 students in each class. In the summer between semesters for a six week period I taught school cafeteria employees how to take advantage of using government surplus food to cut costs. Items were surplus wheat, bulgar flour and salted butter, etc.

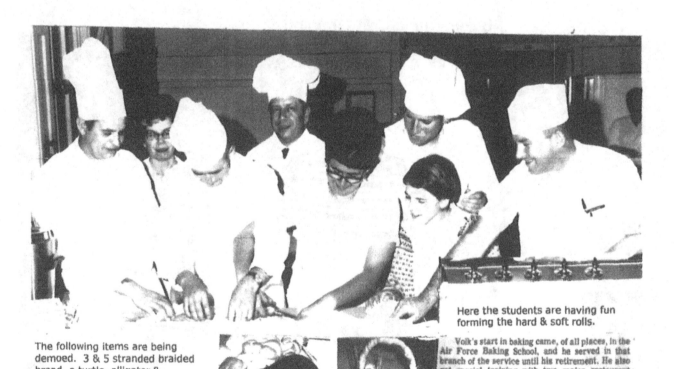

Here the students are having fun forming the hard & soft rolls.

The following items are being demoed. 3 & 5 stranded braided bread, a turtle, alligator & teddy bear. Also how to basket weave over a bowl. Also demoing hard & soft rolls with recipes to take home

Volk's start in baking came, of all places, in the Air Force Baking School, and he served in that branch of the service until his retirement. He also got special training with two major restaurant chains and additional special training at the Waldorf Astoria, Statler Hilton and Governor Clinton hotels in New York City.

Added to that have been special studies with several noted American European chefs.

43

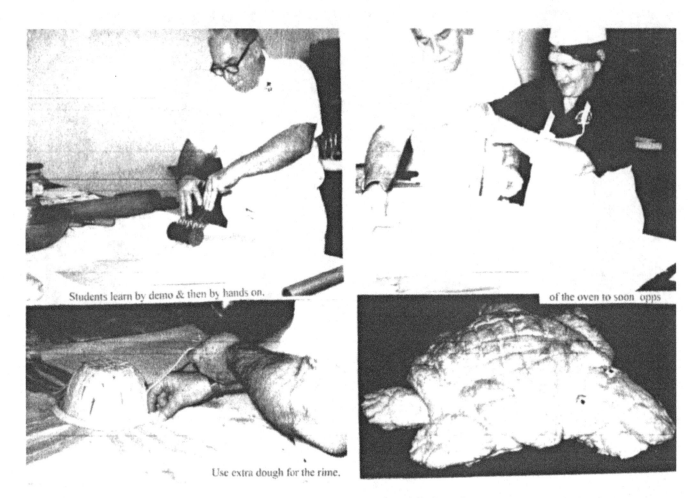

Students learn by demo & then by hands on.

of the oven to soon opps

Use extra dough for the rime.

Bakers Hand Craft Training School.

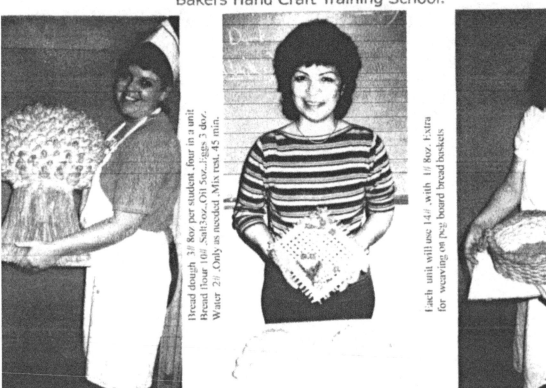

Bread dough 3# 8oz per student ,four in a unit
Bread flour 10# ,Salt3oz.,Oil 5oz.,Eggs 3 doz.
Water 2# ,Only as needed ,Mix rest, 45 min.

Each unit will use 14# ,with 1# 8oz. Extra
for weaving on peg board bread baskets

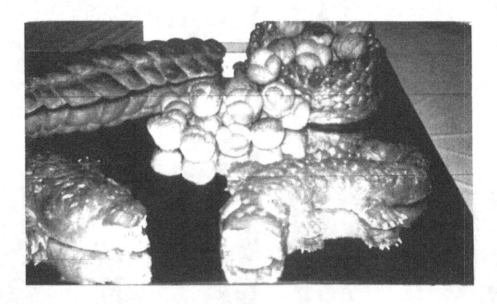

Students worked on these projects with hard roll dough minus the yeast or with tail bread. They were given 3 lbs. 8 oz. to work with.

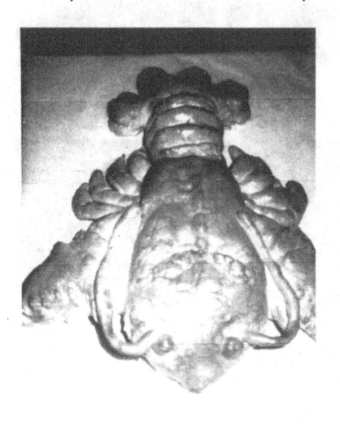

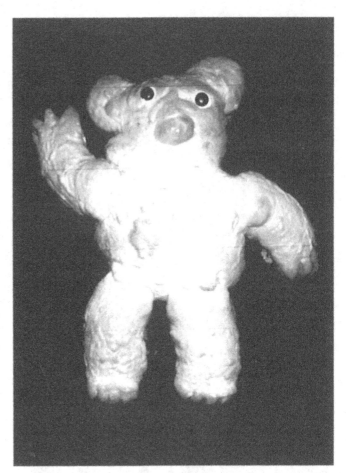

Teddy Bear 3lbs. 8 oz.
Body   1 lb. 4 oz.
Arms & Legs 1 lb. 2 oz.
Head   10 oz.
Ears   5 oz.
Nose & Belly Button
                      3 oz.
Put together with egg whites

Bake with an egg wash,
water & salt.

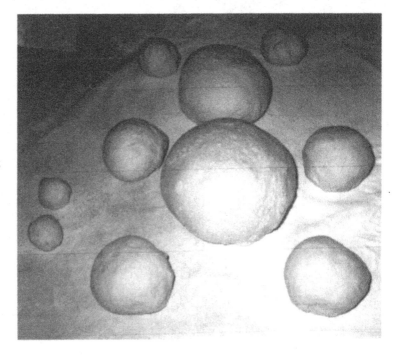

Bakers Hand Craft Training, Learning The Skills Of (Baking & Pastries) (Also) (Cake Decorating) (Tail Bread Art) (Ice Carvings) (Gingerbread houses) (Pulled Sugar)(Entering Culinary Shows) (Etc) For Better Employment, In Hotels, Country Clubs, Catering, Or Starting There Own Business, Latter.

Adolph (Steve) Volk, Instuctor - Certified Culinary Educator and Certified Executive Pastry Chef A.C.F., R.B.A. Master Baker

47

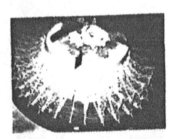

Go To GOOGLE Type In (aolphstevevolk@yahoo.com)
Next (Culinary Olympic)Next(AutherHouse)Next(www
AutherHouse Review The Other Books & Lower Prices

The following photos were taken aboard the Queen Mary, docked at Long Beach CA (1986). Cakes were decorated by members of ICES International and California clubs. plus Fremont Cake club.

Approximately 38 pages of Cakes by ICES & CA Cake Clubs
"Recipes & More" ISBN-978-1-4343-2609-6
Book by AuthorHouse, Phone 1-888-280-7715

Certificate of Achievement recipients, and educators who are committed to furthering their education and enhancing their careers in the restaurant and foodservice industry by awarding scholarships through its Scholarships and Mentoring Program.

Careers & Education

National Restaurant Association Educational Foundation

American Culinary Federation

...geles Mission College

...sion College

...th Team

Nationwide association of professional chefs offers continuing education, apprenticeship training, and scholarships. St. Augustine FL. (800) 624-9458 or (904) 824-4468.

Kitchen 4

United States Air Force

Commendation Medal for Military Merit

SPECIAL ORDER   27 December 1962
G-108

1. In accordance with Department of the Air Force Special Order Number AF-16023, dated 11 December 1962, announcement is made of the retirement of TECHNICAL SERGEANT ADOLPH M. VOLK, JR., AF12256801, 3201st Support Squadron, Air Force Systems Command, Eglin Air Force Base, Florida, effective 31 December 1962, after completing 20 years and 20 days active military service.

2. SERGEANT VOLK was born in Mineola, New York on 25 October 1925. He entered military service on 27 October 1942 and has served overseas in the Asiatic-Pacific Theater of Operations and Alaska.

3. During his long and honorable service, SERGEANT VOLK has earned the following decorations and service awards: Purple Heart, Silver Lifesaving Medal, Air Force Commendation Medal, Commendation Ribbon, Navy Commendation Ribbon with 1 Gold Star, Navy Unit Commendation, Navy Unit Citation, American Campaign Medal, Asiatic-Pacific Campaign Medal with 3 Silver Service Stars and 1 Bronze Service Star, Philippine Liberation Ribbon with 2 Bronze Service Stars, Army of Occupation Medal (Japan), World War II Victory Medal, Navy Good Conduct Medal, Philippine Independence Ribbon, National Defense Service Medal, Air Force Longevity Service Award with 4 Bronze Oak Leaf Clusters, and the Good Conduct Medal with Bronze Clasp, 4 Loops.

4. The Air Proving Ground Center extends best wishes for a happy period of retirement to SERGEANT VOLK.

FOR THE COMMANDER

LEONARD C. HICKS, JR.
Lt Colonel, USAF
Director of Administrative Services

Veterans of Foreign Wars of the United States

REX T. RICE, SR.
POST 67 - 17
SPECIAL ADVISOR ON MILITARY DECORATIONS

CA 95670 5348   (916) 363-8206

100 % Disabled Veteran (W.W.II)
Records > (Mather V.A. Hospital)

Asiatic Pacific Battle Stars
3 Silver Stars (5 each)
1 Bronze Star
16 major battle stars

Philippine Liberation
2 Bronze Stars

While visiting France in 1976, I was informed about The above bake shop that made objects out of tail bread. It was very productive. shipping out orders daily. The founder has since retired and his daughter took over. The bakery was located several miles from the Eiffel Tower.

The daughter, standing behind her father, does much of the work in tail bread. She seems to really enjoy her profession.

Novelty Bread

Bread Flour	10#	
Salt		2oz.
Sugar		1oz.
Milk Powder		2oz.
Yeast Dry		2oz.
Warm Water	4#	8oz.
Total Weight	14#	15oz.

Noodle Bread

Bread Flour	5#	
Eggs (16)	1#	8oz.
Salt		2oz.
Veg. Oil		1oz.
Water	1#	
Total Weight	7#	11oz.

Hard Roll Dough

Bread Flour	5#	
Salt		2oz.
Sugar		2oz.
Veg. Shortening		2oz.
Egg Whites		2oz.
Warm Water	3#	
Yeast		2oz.
Total Weight	8#	11oz.

When touring bake shops in Europe I came across these dough dollies. I bought the girl and butterfly and the man with the bird.

Salt Dough

Bread Flour	4 cups
Salt	1 cup
Water	12oz.

Loaf Bread Dough

White Loaf	1#
Remove the Crust	
Elmers Glue	5oz.

Above sculptures made from salt block.   Castle below I believe is from noodle dough.

Union Helvetia Hotel Restaurant
cooking and pastry classes.
Sr. students will enter the Jr.
Culinary Olympics.

55

Culinary students from around the world participating in the 1988 Culinary Olympics, Frankfurt, Germany, which is held every four years. It is an honor for them to compete with fellow students. Competition will sharpen their skills for future events and boost their careers as professionals.

Military Teams cook under conditions similar to Military Exercises or Operations.

Students at work, bonding a friendship of peace. All below the age of 23.

Youth Participants in front of the audience and judges.

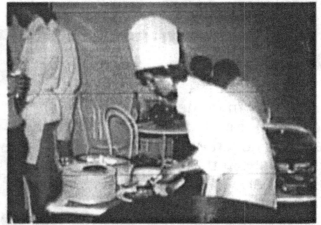

From all over the world at the National Youth Teams competition.

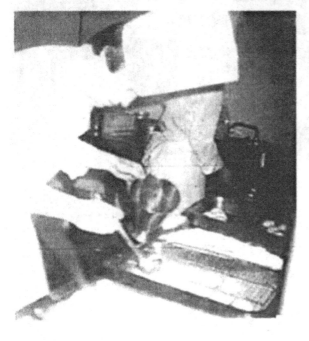

Judges assess technical skills
and creative presentat

This bakery in Rome has been in the family for more than four generations. Note the old light in the upper right corner. I photographed a few of the letters sent to them over the years.

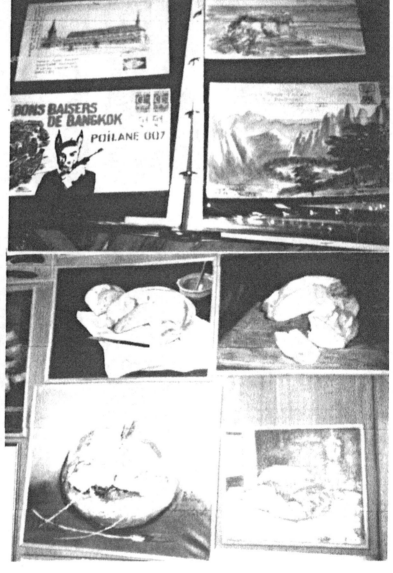

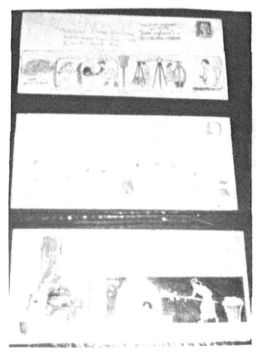

Bread bakery is two floors underground. Bakers work in shorts & sandels.

This wood comes down a shoot twice a day.

I am looking at this very old brick oven. It is very hot down in this bread bakery. Owner explaining how bread is shipped in trucks, planes and trains.

Pets are welcome in bakeries an coffee houses
Bread and apple pastries are the main bakery items.

2ⁿᵈ Bake shop in Rome Italy.

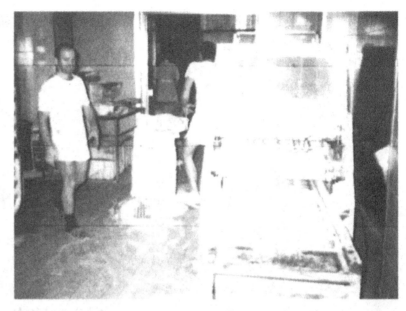

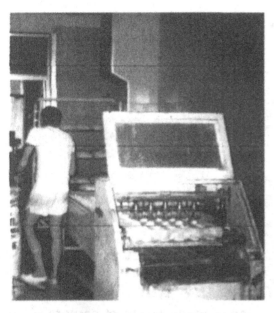

3rd Bake shop, their major items are apple pastries. Average 600 per hour.

This is one of many areas where apprentice bakers are working on filling the dough with apples.

Buy it fresh and hot, street sales.   4th Retail bakery, one of many on street corners.

5th You can buy your bread out of the basket. Bring your shopping bag.

6th Bakery owner showing me his oven. 7th Fine Pastry & Coffee shop/a dozen more to go.

These championship ice carvings were done in Salt Lake City UT. Note: Magazines interested in any photos for reproduction, please contact www.adolphstevevolk@yahoo.com. To order photos please contact my email.

National Restaurant Assn., sponsors chef's competition. Chefs are graded on timing, quality and presentation, and always under pressure to do their best.

Judges keep score by checking quality and presentation. The difficult part of judging is that only a few winners are selected for medals. But lessons are learned from errors and challenges.

More and more bakery retailers are getting involved with community activities and charities. Steve Volk of Volk's Cake & Cooky Co., CA was roped into the project of assisting in the creation of the world's largest dessert for Martini & Rossi's fourth annual Dessert Day. Very often self employed bakery owners, instructors and hotels are "invited" to participate in community activities and donate their goods and time to charity. The gratification received is believing in the worth while cause to those you are donating your time and efforts.

If asked to participate in a project in which travel is involved it helps to make reservations, hotel and airline, through a travel agent. Our favorite is AAA Travel. Make sure the promoter and you have an agreement that your travel expenses will be reimbursed. Stay on good terms with all people involved.

Check on supplies and tools you will need. You know your business, the promoter doesn't. Best helpers are often students from a nearby culinary school and their instructor. Plan ahead. DO NOT try to do a large project on your own.

Icing on the cake, Guiness Book of Records style

MODERN BAKING JANUARY 1994

Well over 45 tables line the walls with chefs from Chicago, showing appetizers and desserts from their respective hotels. The entrance fee was costly, the proceeds going to local charities. Food, wine and labor were all donated.

CHEF CURTIS FLEHARTY
Culinary Educator

ADOLPH (Steve) VOLK, A.C.F.
Certified Executive Pastry Chef

A pound cake which was to be the world's largest dessert for Martini & Rossi on National Dessert Day 1995. A successful fund raiser.

Alva & Susan

Our wives, our support: Alva Volk & Susan Fleharty

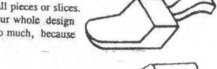

FIRST ROUGH CUTS Regardless of the way you mark the rough outline on the surface of the soap, your next step is to make your first rough cuts, removing the greater part of the soap which will not be used to carve your design. Place the soap on the table or tray, and holding it with the left hand, start cutting at the upper right-hard corner, leaving about 1/4" margin outside your outline or penciled sketch. Cut clear through the cake, removing excess soap all the way around. After making these first cuts, you will probably find it more comfortable to hold the piece in your hand. Continue to carve along your outline, using the knife as if peeling a potato. Keep 1/8" to 1/4" away from your guide lines to allow for finer work later.

CAUTION In roughing out, cut away in small pieces or slices. Soap often breaks if cut in big chunks, and your whole design might be spoiled. Cut too little rather than too much, because you cannot put back a piece once it is cut off.

SHAPING THE MODEL Round out your design by cutting around the corners. As you work, keep turning the soap, always keeping the shape of the piece in mind. Watch your high points -- those that jut out farthest from the surface -- and your low points -- those farthest in. Carve gradually from the high points toward the deepest cuts. It may help to use your knife point in some of this work. Keep observing the whole form as you work at each part. Don't try to finish any one part in detail before another.

CARVINGS WITH SIMPLE PLANES ARE BEST FOR BEGINNERS.........

YOUR IDEA Your subject is often suggested by the shape and quality of the soap. Don't be too ambitious at first. Choose a simple design with a solid, basic shape, without too many delicate undercuts or projections.

DETAILS When the piece is about finished and all planes and forms shaped, you can smooth rough edges with the edge of the knife and mark in details like eyes or ears, etc., with the knife tip or with your orangewood stick.

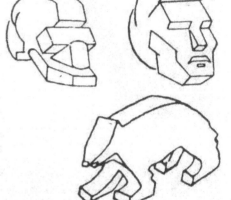

PREPARING THE SOAP It's best to unwrap the soap and allow it to dry for a day before you start carving. Cut away the raised edges; scrape off the lettering. You'll have a beautiful flat surface for your carving. Carving on a tray will keep everything ship-shape and make it easy to collect the chips.

TO POLISH First, allow the model to dry for a day or two. Then, rub it with a soft paper napkin, being careful not to break off corners or projections. Finally, rub it gently with finger tips or palm.

THE TOOLS Your medium and tools are simple and inexpensive: a large cake of white soap (Ivory's shape and texture are most satisfactory); a paring knife; one or two "manicure" orangewood sticks. Pencil and paper for sketching will help.

FROM IDEA TO SOAP If you have a clear mental picture of your idea, you can carve directly in the soap, or you may use the orangewood stick to outline a rough sketch on all surfaces of the form you wish to carve. Beginners may wish to sketch ideas on a piece of paper first, then transfer it to the soap by tracing or by using carbon paper.

This "walk-thru" wedding cake was most challenging. The bride
wanted to be able to walk under her cake. If you are interested in
doing one, two stainless pipes run through two 55 gallon barrels.
Holding up the top of the cake is a ¾ inch plywood board. The guests
were flown in from various parts of the country. The Italian dinner
was the best I have ever eaten. Quite the wedding.

This Certificate is Awarded

T/Sgt Adolph Volk

in Recognition of Distinguished Service

To the Men and Women

of America's Armed Forces through the

United Service Organizations, Inc.

Edwin E. Bond
EXECUTIVE DIRECTOR

Harvey S. Firestone Jr.
NATIONAL CHAIRMAN

CHAIRMAN, LOCAL USO COMMITTEE

PRESIDENT

February 21, 1962

★ www.uso.org

TELL US YOUR USO STORY

When I was active in the service the USO served as an organization that offered comfort to us servicemen on the move. Small things such as a donut and cup of coffee and often a sandwich while we were on a stop over in a new location. There were times while waiting for a flight at the airport that there was a lounge for our comfort. Which reminded us a little of the comforts of home and always snacks provided that were always appreciated. GI's always seemed to have huge appetites.

When we arrived at the port in Los Angeles we again stopped at the USO lounge. The volunteers serving sandwiches that day were Shirley Temple Black and Judy Garland. That was a special bonus for us, quite a treat.

My payback was having the privilege of decorating a cake for a special event of the USO. Thanks for the "memories".

You may also mail submissions and agreements to: Emily Swanson, USO World Headquarters, 2111 Wilson Blvd, Suite 1200, Arlington, Va. 22201.

The delicious aroma of fresh cinnamon rolls baking
was an invitation to stop by and savor every bite.
We enjoy this particular item each year we attend the
California State Fair in Sacramento.   We watch them
mix the dough, then placing it on the bench ready to
roll out. They are coated with butter, and a mixture of
cinnamon and sugar, then the dough is rolled up and cut,
and placed into pans ready to rise. After the bake off
they are coated with icing. There is always a line at
this booth. They are soooo good...

REQUEST FOR DONATION OR ADVERTISEMENT

Requests for donations and advertisements have become so numerous that we have designed this form as a means to fairly allocate our budgeted donations and advertising allowance. Thank you for your cooperation.

If Merchandise Donation: (specify) ☐ Gift Certificate ☐ ¼ sheet Cake Value $ _____

⦙ Boxes MUST be checked for processing ☐ Cookies ☐ Other _____

If Advertisement: Name of Publication: _____

Publication Date _____ Coverage # _____ Area _____ Cost of Ad $_____

Cake Dummy: (Size) ☐ Two Tier ☐ Three Tier Color of Flowers _____

Has your organization received donations from us in the past? ( ) YES ( ) NO

If Yes, when 1/_____ ;2/_____ ;3/_____. Is organization non-profit? ( ) YES ( ) NO

Purpose for which donation will be used _____

Purpose for which money raised will be used _____

President/Head of Organization: _____ Phone: _____

Address: _____

Person making request: _____ Phone: _____

Address: _____

Are you a customer in our shop? ( ) YES ( ) NO For how long? _____

How often? _____ Last two purchases: Dates _____ _____

Have other bakeries been contacted for this request? ( ) YES ( ) NO

Are other businesses being contacted for this request? ( ) YES ( ) NO

If yes, which ones? Name _____ Phone: _____

Name _____ Phone: _____

Name _____ Phone: _____

In order to be fairly processed, this request must be filled out and returned

Name _____

Title _____

Date(s) Needed: _____ _____

Company _____

Address _____

City _____ State _____ Zip _____

Phone _____

What category best describes your operation?	Check all that apply.	
Business/Industry ....☐	Recreational Facility..........☐	Hospital/Nursing Home ....☐
Casual/Theme...............☐	Retail Store ....☐	Hotel/Motel/Resort............☐
Contract Feeder.............☐	School/College..............☐	Military/Government...........☐

This form was set up for people wanting donations. It seems that when you are in business you become a target from people who often do not otherwise patronize your shop but will contact you regarding a donation, year after year.